THE UP-RISING IN DYING

Pensive and faltering, the word "the Dead" I write;
For living are the dead;
Haply the only living, only real,
And I the apparition — I the spectre.

Walt Whitman

THE UP-RISING IN DYING

WORDS AND VERSES

for those close to the experience
surrounding
The Threshold of Death

Edited by
Christy Barnes & Janet Hutchinson

A Collection for Individual Use
or for the Forming of Festivals

ADONIS PRESS
HAWTHORNE VALLEY
GHENT, NEW YORK

Cover by Van James

ACKNOWLEDGMENTS

The editors would like to thank the Anthroposophic Press for permission to reprint pages 125-228 from *The Mission of the Archangel Michael* by Rudolf Steiner, and for Arvia Ege's translations of verses by Rudolf Steiner from *Truth-Wrought-Words*, 1979. They are also grateful to Sandra Sherman for her proof reading and advice.

ISBN: 0-932776-16-7

Second Printing, 1994

FOREWORD

There is a new kind of awareness of the nature of death in the world today, and at the same time a growing need to find the means to deal with the suffering, loss and questions which it stirs within us. We feel this when we are confronted with the death of children as well as of the very old and those suddenly taken in youthful years. And the question arises, "Is there a way I can help those who have already died?"

There have been important break-throughs in the knowledge about death during this century: earlier through Rudolf Steiner's spiritual-scientific research and more recently, through their experiences with the dying, of such pioneers as Elizabeth Kubler-Ross and others. And now through the selfless work of innumerable hospice volunteers, a growing helpfulness and skill of heart in dealing with terminal illness is spreading throughout society.

This book has arisen out of the wish to serve this growing awareness and need, and out of the conviction that poetry has the subtlety, imagination and heart forces to illuminate the mystery and stature of this universal event and to help and give strength and courage to those who approach it. Especially when a poem is learned by heart and so becomes one's own, it can be a constant source of sustaining nourishment.

The poems and prose which have been selected here come from the sources most immediately available to the editors of this volume, and so many of them have arisen out of the individual experiences of a very limited number of people. We hope that nevertheless they may have a universal helpfulness both to individuals and to communities.

Some of the material was written by experienced seers and poets, other pieces by those of lesser ability out of personal urgency, one of these on page 55, by a girl of nineteen upon hearing of the death of an eighty-six-year-old artist whom she knew.

Over a number of years, works which appear here have been used, together with other art forms, to celebrate All Souls Day on November second — that day, following All Hallows and Halloween, traditionally devoted to the memory and thoughts of the dead. These "festivals" can help to heighten the awareness of the connection between the living and the so-called dead in an entire community.

The purpose and wish of the editors is that this book may reach out as far as possible among those of any age, race, and especially of any creed, to whom any part of its contents may become helpful.

The Editors

CONTENTS

TRANSLATORS: *C.B.* Christy Barnes, *V.B.* Virginia Brett, *A.M.E.* Arvia
   MacKaye Ege, *P.M-K.* Percy MacKaye, *L.M.* Lisa Monges.

INTRODUCTION

THE NEEDS AND TASKS
OF THOSE WHO HAVE DIED

In earlier times the relationship between the living and the so-called dead was, in a natural, although not fully conscious way, a much closer one than it is today. The influence of materialism has been to weaken and gradually to sever this bond. But in the future a bridge will be built once again to those who have died, but this time quite consciously. For those who have passed through death need and long for the love and the thoughts of those who were close to them on earth. Although they find themselves surrounded by the light of the spirit, they also need what the living can give them. Yet materialistic thoughts have little reality for them and so do not reach them. Loving, life-filled spiritual thoughts, on the other hand, are like nourishment for them, without which they go hungry. And there is often much hunger of this kind today among those who are experiencing the life after death.

Thus we here can help and work not only for those who live on the earth, but also for the dead, through the life-filled, spirit-filled thoughts which we bring to them.

And on the other hand this relationship is by no means one-sided, and those who have died can in turn be of very real help to the living.

One part of the task of those who have died is that their gaze, their spiritual gaze, now turns toward those who still live upon the earth, so that the souls living upon the earth are perceived by the souls who have died. And through spiritual science men will learn the meaning of such words as these: — "Those who have passed through the portal of death gaze upon me, they imbue me with life, they are with me; their forces stream down upon me." — And men will learn to speak of the dead as ones who live, as spiritually living ones.

Through spiritual science we learn to feel responsible for all that we do in relationship to the dead, but we learn to know also the deep feeling of blessing when we can say to ourselves — "At this moment you are doing one thing or another; but as you do so, one or the other who has died beholds you with his active powers, his forces grow together with your own." — Not that the dead *give* us the forces, these we must develop ourselves. The one who has died, who is between death and a new birth, does not give us our talents: we must have these. But he is a very real and active help, as if he stood there behind us. And indeed he does really stand there behind us. I may be doing this or that, but as I am doing it, one or the other who has died beholds me with his active powers, his forces grow together with my own, streaming into me as a very real and active help as if he stood there behind me.

And indeed we can become aware that the dead are in all reality constantly there, about and behind us.

Rudolf Steiner

I have made ready a room
Here in my heart
With walls of warmth
And windows of color
Towards every side of the cosmos.

Oceans, mountains and clouds
Are without;
Within — loving and light;
And here I invite you to come,
Dear being I love.

Lead me in what you have learned
Now you have left your earthly
Body with so long suffering
And become a heavenly star:
The up-rising in dying.

Albert Steffen

ARE YOU THE DEAD?

Are you the dead
Who hover like soft sunlight
Round my bed,

Who warm the gloom
And flood with tender quietude
This chill, dark room,

And did you start
This silent flow of peace
Within my heart?

Oh, is it you
Whom I so dearly love
And dearly knew.

Are you the dead?
"Oh no — love does not die,
We live!" they said.

Arvia MacKaye Ege

6

THE MYSTERY OF DEATH

In the calm of night skies
The River of Death flows
    over the star bed of Heaven
In cascades of light.

                    Eleanor Trives

A never-ceasing sense of thankfulness towards all human beings lives in the heart — for all of them make a contribution to the development of mankind that no one else can make, in that they carry their destiny, whatever it may be, through to the end.

They take themselves through birth into life and yet know that they must endure death. And each death is a life-achievement, is personally different for each personality and so of inestimable value. And from each death another can learn. And each crossing of the threshold is a *deed*.

Albert Steffen
From an unpublished notebook

Death is that inexorable instant of life
That demonstrates life's infinite dignity
Under all trivial forms — the lightning knife
That cuts them to their great core, cleansingly.
In death God builds the gods their inner shrine;
Because of death we know we are divine.

Percy MacKaye

Are we not all woven like bright blossoms
With strands of light into one flowering wreath —
Those of us who breathe the breath of heaven
And those who breathe the naked air beneath.

So like one unfading cosmic garland,
So firmly, ever newly intertwined,
We weave the life-web of the seamless garment
Of the spirit being of mankind.

Arvia MacKaye Ege

Death and birth
Create and devastate the earth.
Birth and death
Give both soul and spirit breath.

For life is dying into death,
Death arising into life,
And in between, the human heart,
That bleeds for both in mortal strife
To hold and harmonize the two,
Receives the sustenance of art —
The secret ever forged anew.

Arvia MacKaye Ege

Dear death is a doorway
From night into light,
From weight to the height,
From search into sight —
A heart-guarded archway
From earth to new birth.

Arvia MacKaye Ege

There is no other star like you, O sun,
So full of love, so full of life and light.
Could any other body shine as bright,
Or gently warm like you, O heavenly one?
Poised in yourself upon your cosmic run,
Without comparison in godly might,
Your constant presence is our dearest sight.
Oh do not leave us when our days are done!

When we have woken from our world of dreams,
Then let us see you as you really are,
As radiant raiment of the living Christ,
And fill our souls with your aetherial streams,
That we can also learn to be a star
In higher worlds where you are the All High'st.

Rex Raab

Ye who have entered into Timelessness,
Oh, let us with your light of soul discern
In your great realm the images to fill
Earth-seeming with Divine Reality!

Let us transform all dazzle to gold-of-heart,
Transmute all shadow into blue of heaven,
Win understanding from the wilderness,
And find a home in the forsaken places.

Where — at the setting of our earthly sun —
We see the Light of Life in resurrection
By the stone slab, that lay upon the grave,
Become the altar where the Christ awaits us —

And, being quickened by His Bread of Life
And Spirit Wine, gaze backward, far along
The earthly way below, where once we wandered
between the portals of our death and birth

And find again all that we lost, till even
Out of our very wounds our healing flows,
And pains of exhaustion turn to exaltations
That glorify the doom which makes us human.

Imagining now the plan of our new house
Framed all for offerings to our nobler being —
Its earthy door high coped with spirit-towers,
Vaulted with stars, arcaded with the sun-gold —

We now erect the mansion of our body
Wherein all newly we descend to earth:
Oh, aid us in the building of that temple!
Oh, help us work deep in the deeds of earth!

Albert Steffen

He who had died and loved me, held his hand
Before my mouth and only said, "Be still."
And after the long suffering, my will
Grew, brimming to my eyes in new command,

And I saw deeper than I saw by day.
The Word that was denied me became sight;
And what was robbed from me returned in light.
When gods are near, no life can pass away.

Ah, have you ever worked for harm or fear?
Then seek the guiding word of one who died.
Who heals another heals himself beside.
The spirit's birth begins with dying here.

Albert Steffen

Only
the lonely
are led
to the threshold
of sight.

Only
the dead
can tread
the ocean
of light.

Only
the living
are fed
the bread
of the night.

Arvia MacKaye Ege

DEATH AS EXPERIENCED
BY THE LIVING

MEDITATION AT THE DEATH
OF A FRIEND

Death came to him, they say,
that moment when the shuddering sleeper tossed
his last moist, life-drenched, pain-wrenched breath
back to the stars, and air no longer streamed
in sounding harmonies on red-blood-beating wings,
when rhythmic-pounding earth-drum answered stillness
        with a hush,
its earth-psalm ceased.

And that was death. The pallid, moon-white sibyl crept,
her clutching fingers twisting off the roses,
to reveal black beams that bear the milk-white marble
        luminous aloft.
A soft light shimmers on the silent sleeper's brow,
but all the roses have been plucked and pilfered now.

Ah, but behold the marble marvel.
There is beauty in this deftly chiselled stone.
What hands have carved and cut this graven, fine-etched
        form?
It lies there still and sacred, delicate as ivory and deep,
        mysterious.
Who held the mallet and what blows of fate have given it
        force?
It was strong speech that has in-formed this stone!

And you, my friend, you've borne the hammering words
       through many winters.
You have been the stone. The artist's work is finished.
Though the stuff shall crumble, yet these furrowed lines
       of human face and form
speak of the sculpted masterpiece that shall endure
       the storm.

You lie there silent, and I know
that I am in the presence of a mystery.
This hollow, cast-off shell betrays its secret,
speaks of him who lived and loved there once
and was the light that dwelt within its walls,
enduring them, refurnishing them, until —
lone traveller on a star-drenched sea —
he cast that shell off, left his silent tower,
and leapt from limits to the All,
from skull to sky, from shell to vast, celestial sphere.

What then is death? Your quiet corpse bears eloquent
       witness to the ways of earth.
Now I must turn my vision toward the light.
Not from that black box there, but in the syllables of
       soaring flight
your Spirit leaps and laughs at me.
You always were, you are and you shall be!
"Christ rules the living and the dead.
His Kingdom is the shining mansion of Eternity!"

                                        Michael Burton

17

So suddenly you went
To join the living dead,
While there was still so much unsaid,
So many hopes unsolved,
Such human store unspent,
that the gaping rent
Your leaving left within my heart
Has torn the kernel of my self apart
And laid it open to the quick —
Bared, down to its quivering core
The hidden fibers and the bleeding flesh
Of those soul substances which weave
The whole great, pulsing mortal mesh
Of our immortal destiny,
All wounded, raw —

Yet there,
At the very quick of such despair,
With piercing certainty, I see,
Heart-rendingly,
How, through the anguish of the wound,
Its all-engulfing pain —
Like the swift, fusing mystery of flame
Lifting from the crumbling ash
In clarifying light —
By such burning change, we wake
To glimpse — and then partake
Of a love more free, more clear,
More near, revealing, dear —

Deepening more
And ever more...
Than on the earth
We could have known
Before.

Arvia MacKaye Ege

O MY ANGEL

O my Angel, spread your wings
And bear me to the source of things —

Far into the world of light
Hidden in the heart of night.

O my Angel, let me sleep —
Bathe me in the star-bright deep.

Bathe my being bright and clean —
Heal me in the vast unseen.

Arvia MacKaye Ege

PAIN

Until we learn to bear
Some small heart-rending share
of the Saviour's suffering,
We will never find the cure
For man's ultimate despair.

Unless we can endure
The piercing touch of His pierced hand,
We will not waken to the light
That streams with freeing healing
From the spirit land.

Until we can perceive, suffer and believe
Some vestige of the vast
Incredibly true story
That breathes within each brother's hidden plight,

Can cherish and forgive
The pain and strife —
The budding life
Its emerging mystery creates,

We will never grasp
What all the mortal suffering this great earth o'er
Is for —
The future kingdom
Gleaming at its core —

That warming morning glory —
That quenchless flow
Of sun-insight —

The tender surety,
The all-trusting purity,
Of love's fair, foundless, all-availing might! —

Arvia MacKaye Ege

Joy and sadness keep so near;
courage thrives so close to fear;
comfort comes to darkest hours:
thus decree the highest powers.
Fear and sadness last a day;
courage, joy and comfort stay.

Rex Raab

For Mary Louise and Ralph Bedard,
who lost their child after a few weeks.

21

CARDIOGRAPH

In intensive care.

The undulations of the cardiograph,
deciphering the heart-beat's each degree,
are but a far-off, ghostly epitaph
to life-blood in its true reality.

Embedded in the waves of cosmic time,
that lap the shores of earth and universe,
the human pulse is part of a sublime,
poetic, living, heart-inspiring verse.

Its melodies and rhythms are the dance
of sungods guiding stars and moon and earth
to rest beneath the godhead's countenance,
flushed by the sunrise of its own rebirth.

Rex Raab

Alone — No answer. — Silence terrible
    As blindness' stare: silence more dark
Than fog-born cataracts, dumbed by sudden lull
    In Abyssinian mountains: muteness, stark

As terror, but mightier with pregnant peace
    Than pain etherialized. — Alone: alone
As Psyche, listening where all melodies cease.
    No answer: — only that tegument of tone

Chiselled to silence ... till — with instant glow
    Articulate — Christ of the sealéd lips
You spoke, at last! Out of the dark of woe
    Upward, roundward, sundering the dumb eclipse,

Your Wonder called, as when some thunder-quake
Shudders the world, and all its kingdoms shake.

Percy MacKaye

IN CANDLE-LIGHT

Commanding was the courage of her face,
sculptured by the frozen tides of death,
image of inexorable truth —
immensely strong and resolutely brave....

A pansy lay between her folded hands,
upon her breast a simple crucifix.
Flowering hawthorn and forget-me-nots
nestled on the snow-white coverlet.
Lilies of the valley, tiny lilies,
then we laid like clustering stars about her,
close about her head, about her shoulders,
all their little shining bells entwining
mid the silvery ringlets of her hair,
peonies, like dawn-clouds, at her feet.

See — in the sheltering candle-shine — she smiles!
Gracious peace has stolen o'er her face,
growing ever deeper, gentler, brighter
as the hours take their silent pace....

And a second night again we robed her,
robed her for the heavens once again.
How the lilies of the valley sparkled
like a sea of stars about her head —
ringing all their little bells in chorus,
ringing: "Risen — risen — she is risen!..."

All the while, amid the candle-glow,
what majestic transformation moved
with mysterious might across her face!
Like a Grecian hero, as of old —
her wondrous hair, like clouds of mystery
and glory, sweeping upward from her brow —
it seemed she strode with eager virgin vigor
over mountain-tops at break of day,
only soon to nestle once again
close into the flowers' quiet clasp
so tenderly, with such unfathomed peace —

When all at once, as night was swiftly passing,
she grew so young! — and ever sweetly younger.
Her eye-lids seemed to flicker and to lift,
and like a sudden flash of spirit lightning,
as clear as heaven's fire, she looked at us —
although her frozen lids were ever husht:
a glad young goddess, gracious and serene,
the cross that leads to life upon her heart —
reflecting here her bright eternal being
that rose above in light and majesty
about to start upon its starward way,
to wander forth into the fields of love — —
out into the pastures of the Day....

Arvia MacKaye Ege

FOR A CHILD
WHO FEARS DEATH

Christ is here,
I feel and see
His warm bright sunlight
Shine in me.

He shines away
The night of fear.

Christ is here.
I feel and see
His warm bright sunlight
Shine in me.

Christy Barnes

26

INTO GOD'S DAY

Whom you seek, he is not here
Where our weeping is.
He who breathes the light as his
Has no grave to fear.

One who rose from death to birth
Broke His tomb apart.
None who holds Him in his heart
Hides in walls of earth.

Fling the rigid shroud-cloth wide
As eagle wings! Take breath:
Rise up from the hill of death
On the spirit's tide.

Lay the old long ache away.
Kneel not with earth's woe.
Praise the Gods! Let grieving go.
Stride into God's day!

Albert Steffen

Wonder ever,
Cease love never,
Then the breath
Of Death
Need never
Sever.

No, not ever.

C. B.

DEATH
AS EXPERIENCED BY THOSE
WHO HAVE CROSSED THE THRESHOLD

THE MOMENT OF DEATH —
SEEN FROM THE OTHER SIDE

...As little as man, living on earth and looking back to the moment of birth, can ever perceive his own birth, as little as this experience ever stands before the ordinary forces of the soul (there is no man who can, through ordinary soul forces, look back to his physical birth), just as necessary is it that there is always the moment of death to which one looks back. Death always stands there as the last significant event. This death, seen from the other side, from beyond death, is something totally different from what is seen from the physical side. It is the most beautiful experience that can be seen from the other side, from the side of life between death and rebirth. It appears as the glorious picture of the eternal victory of the spirit over matter. And it is therefore, because it appears as such a picture, the constant awakener of the highest forces in man, while he is dwelling in spirit-experience between death and rebirth.

Rudolf Steiner

THE ONE WHO HAS DIED
SPEAKS

In radiant light
'Tis there I feel
The power of life.
For death
Has wakened me from sleep —
From spirit sleep.

Oh, I shall be
And do from out me
What radiant power
Within me shines.

I was united with you,
So remain united in me.
Together we shall speak
The speech of eternal being.
Together we shall act
Where the results of the deeds are at work.
Together we shall weave in spirit,
Where human thought is woven
In the Word of eternal thought.

UNBORN CHILD

From the radiant one,
The sun,
Through the rainbow
Down the sky
I came with flower
And butterfly,
But blossomed not
Upon the earth —
Slipped all at once
Through death and birth
And budded back
Into the glow
And colors of the shining bow,
Building of its light
A home
Up from your hearts
To heaven's dome.

Tend and rock me
Where I lie
In the vastness of the sky.
Where your quiet souls are wed,
Tuck up and watch
My starry bed
Till your two hearts cradle me
In their beating
Lovingly.

Christy Barnes

IN THE PROVINCE
OF CHILDREN'S SOULS

A child who had died found that his cradle, that is to say his coffin (such mistakes are understandable) was too small to lie in. His hands and feet hit against the sides, and so he wanted to get up and look for a more comfortable bed. Raising himself up in his little shirt, he discovered that he was standing in a garden landscape. Flowerbed ranged upon flowerbed. Many boys and girls wandered about through various districts, each according to his liking, now among bluebell blossoms, now purple violets, now through golden lilies.

A larger child stepped up to the smaller one and taught him how to take apart the shrine in which he had lain. The many little sticks of which it was made, he put together crosswise so as to form a fence.

It was astonishing that so tiny a coffin could provide the countless number of little pickets with which an endless region could be encompassed.

Albert Steffen

FOR A SINGER

This is the body I formed,
And I give it back to the earth.
This is the form that I
And the Maker of Music have moulded,
And I have made it sing
With the holy music of heaven.

I leave my body behind
And lifted in light I wing
Like a song up into the ringing
Realms where the Hierarchies hold me,
And the thoughts of your hearts enfold me.

This is the form I let fall
Like a petal back to the earth,
Carven with patience and pain,
Fashioned, life-tested and finished
While I blossom on to rebirth.

Christy Barnes

VERSES AND PROSE PASSAGES
BY RUDOLF STEINER

Spirit of your soul, great active guardian,
May your swinging pinions bring
Our souls' entreating love
To the human being of the spheres
Entrusted to your care.

That united with your power
Our entreaty stream with help
To the soul whom lovingly we seek.

The love of my soul
Is striving to you.
My love's pure sensing
Is streaming to you.
May they bear you aloft
And uphold you there,
In hope's wide heights,
In love's clear spheres.

Into spirit pastures I will send
The faithful love which here we found
That we might be united soul with soul.
So may you find my thinking ever loving
When from the spirit's light-filled lands
You, searching, turn your gaze of soul
To see what here in me you seek.

In the light of world-all thoughts,
There weaves the soul, who
Was united with me on earth.

*

The warm life of my heart
Flows out to your soul,
To warm your cold,
To soothe your heat.
In the spirit worlds
May my thoughts live within thine,
And your thoughts within mine.

Angeloi, Archangeloi, Archai
Receive in the ether's weaving
Your web of destiny.

There pass over
in Exusiai, Dynamis, Kyriotetes
within the astral feeling of the cosmos
the rightful fruits
of your earthly life.

There are resurrected
in Thrones, Cherubim, Seraphim
as substance of their deeds
the rightful deeds
with which you shaped
your earthly life.

The name of the one who has died may, if it is wished,
be spoken at the end of each stanza.

WORDS BY RUDOLF STEINER
Arranged for the Service
for Sophie Stinde

We know what moved you in spirit;
We are feeling what warmed your heart;
We are striving for what impelled your will.

> The impulse of your spirit,
> The warmth of your heart,
> The urgency of your will
> > Stand before our souls.

And remembrance takes shape before us:
> of how you have thought with us
> > what we deemed the worthiest thought-content;
> of how you felt with us
> > what we deemed the purest love of our hearts;
> of how you strove with us
> > for what we deemed mankind's truest aims.

And remembrance is joined by vision of spirit:
> how you are received
> > by the beings of light-filled heights
> > > to work actively in spirit;
> > > to behold the results of your deeds;
> > > to speak the language of eternal life.

Weave* in your active life in spirit,
behold the results of your deeds,
let penetrate into the language of eternal life
        the radiance
        which can penetrate our hearts,
        and which rays back to you
      so that in future times
      we can live a spirit life
        united with you.

The Dead answers:

I (We were) was united with you,
So remain united in me (us).
Together we shall speak
The speech of eternal being.
Together we shall act
Where the results of the deeds are at work,
Together we shall weave in spirit,
Where human thought is woven,
In the Word of eternal thought.

O ye beings in light-filled heights,
      let us treasure
      in boundless spirit-realms
      What has united us here
        in earthly spaces.

*A name may be spoken here: Weave, O _____,

WHAT THE MEMORIES OF THE LIVING MEAN TO THE SOULS OF THE DEAD

If we go into a graveyard and see the people gathered there, filled with the images of their dearly loved dead, and then we look aloft to the souls of those who are being remembered, we can know that these memories are for the dead like beautiful cathedrals — like their great works of art. What streams up to them from the earth illuminates the world for them just as a dearly loved and valued picture calls up the presence of a beloved human being, or just as, here on earth, a magnificent cathedral speaks to us of lofty mysteries in such a way that the world is filled through and through with light. Desolate and empty is the world into which the dead constantly have to gaze unless, out of the souls of those who live here, there rises up to them something that, it seems, is not yet present, but must become present there: the thoughts that unite us who live here upon earth with those who are living in the spirit.

Through this, a deeply moving contrast reveals itself to us — the difference between earthly life and life in the spirit. In order to heighten and elevate earthly life, we must add to it in picture form something new that does not yet exist there. An earth stripped of everything that men can add to it in pictorial form — how desolate that would be!

And now let us raise ourselves to the viewpoint of the dead. They can perceive the constantly evolving spiritual process, but it would be just as desolate and empty for them as imageless nature would be for the children of the earth if our remembrances of them did not remain alive, if unfailing thoughts and remembrances of them were not present — thoughts that are for them like our works of art in as much as they are beautiful thoughts — thoughts that are not entangled with what is only earthly, but directed towards those who no longer live in the processes of the earth.

What here on earth makes a painting or statue truly into a work of art is far less significant, far less connected with the innermost core of human beings, than all that our thoughts can mean for the dead in the spiritual world. For there is also beauty in the spiritual world, a real true beauty; but it arises not so much through what is outward, as it so often does in the physical world — not so much through what appears externally in the form of a picture, for instance.

That the paintings of Raphael, Leonardo and Dürer are more beautiful than those of others is due to the fact that these masters had greater abilities than other masters. That one who has died experiences a more beautiful "work of art" — as one might call it — streaming up towards him from the earth is due to the depth, the inwardness, the holy, spiritual feeling of the memory which we constantly cherish of him. The strength of our perceptive feeling for the dead lays hold upon the life of our souls and deepens it in the presence of the dead themselves. And this makes our souls, too, more and more beautiful.

THE RELATIONSHIP BETWEEN THE LIVING AND THE DEAD

The relationship between the living and those who have died is especially strong at the moment of falling asleep and at the moment of waking up. In reality, every human being poses countless questions and gives information to his beloved dead at the moment of falling asleep and receives messages and answers from them at the moment of waking up. This intercourse with the dead, however, may be cultivated in a certain way....

There is a certain difference in regard to the thoughts which will lead us to a relation with one who has died at the moment of falling asleep; not every thought is equally suitable. Anyone who does not merely lead a sensual-egotistical life will out of a healthy feeling, have the longing not to interrupt the relation which karma has brought him with certain personalities who have now passed through the portal of death. He certainly will frequently connect his thoughts with these personalities. And the thoughts which we connect with our conception of the departed personalities may produce an actual intercourse with the dead, even though we are unable to pay attention to what happens at the moment of falling asleep. Certain thoughts, however, are more favorable than others for such an intercourse. Abstract thoughts, thoughts which we form with a certain indifference, even perhaps only from a sense of duty, are little suited to pass over to the dead at the moment of falling asleep. But thoughts, concepts, which arise from the experience of a special interest which united us in life are well suited to pass over to the dead. If we remember the one who has died in such a way that we do not merely think of him with abstract thoughts and cold concepts, but recall a moment when we grew warm at his side, when he told us something dear to our heart: if we remember the moments we have lived through with him in a community of feeling, and in a community of willing; if we remember the times we undertook and decided something together which we both valued and which led us to a common action — in short, something which made our hearts beat as one; if we recall vividly this mutual beating of our hearts: then all this colors our thought of the departed one so it is able to stream over to him at our next moment of falling asleep. It does not matter whether we have this thought at nine in the morning, at noon, or at two in the afternoon. We may have it at any time during the day: it will remain and stream over to the dead person at the moment of our falling asleep.

At the moment of waking up we may, in turn, receive answers, messages from the departed one. It does not necessarily have to be at the moment of waking up that this arises in our soul, since we may be unable to pay attention to it then; but in the course of the day something may arise in our soul in the form of a good idea, an inspiration, we might say, if we believe in such things. But also in regard to this certain conditions are more favorable, others less so. Under certain conditions it is easier for the dead to find access to our soul. The conditions are favorable if we have acquired a clear conception of the being of the departed one, if we were so deeply interested in his being that it really stood before our spiritual eye. You will ask: Why does he say that? If someone was close to us we certainly have a conception of his being! — I do not believe this at all, my dear friends. People pass one another in our time and know each other very, very little. This may not alienate us from the other being here in the physical world; but it alienates us from the being who dwells in the world of the dead. Here in the physical world there are numerous unconscious and subconscious forces and impulses which bring people close to one another, even though they do not want to learn to know each other. It is supposed to happen in life, as some probably have read, that people may be married for decades and yet have very little knowledge of one another! In such cases the impulses which bring these people together do not rest upon mutual knowledge. Life is permeated everywhere by subconscious or unconscious impulses. These subconscious impulses bind us together here on earth, but they do not bind us to the being who has passed through death before us. In order to effect such a connection it is necessary that we have received into our soul something through which the being of the departed one lives vividly in us. And the more vividly it lives in us, the easier it is for that being to have access to our soul; the easier it is for him to communicate with us.

This is what I wanted to tell you about the intercourse, constantly occurring, between the so-called living and the so-called dead. Every one of us is in constant intercourse with the so-called dead, but the reason we do not know it is that we are unable to observe sufficiently the moment of falling asleep, the moment of waking up. I have told you all this in order to give a more concrete form to your connection with the supersensible world in which the dead dwell.

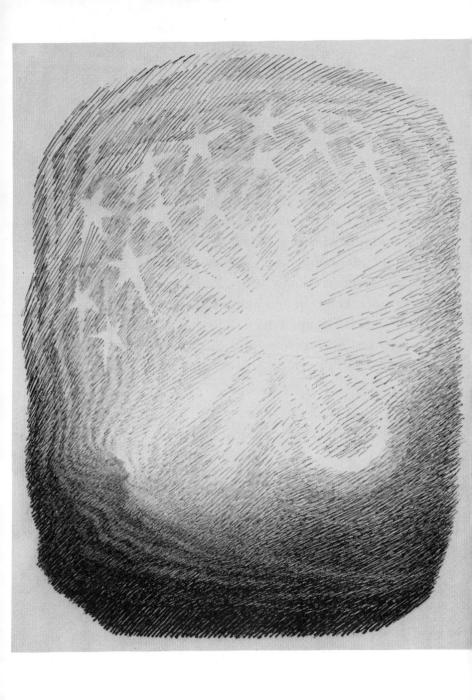

Woodcut

Arvia MacKaye Ege

WORDS OF THE LIVING
FOR THOSE
ON THE OTHER SIDE OF THE THRESHOLD

You who have died and undergone death
With so great suffering
And now look backward,
Rejoicing that you have arisen,
Lend me your strength
That I may lessen
The pain of the living.

Albert Steffen

PASSAGE STARWARD

Beyond the brim of death
Starward now you wander
And stop to hold your breath
As you harken yonder —

The music — hush and listen —
No longer faint remote.
The tones, see how they glisten,
Hear how they peal and float!

"Oh, here 'tis warm and bright
Beyond the veil of seeming,
A land where love and light
Are ever streaming.

Oh, look upon the beauty
Of the human form,
For it is man's duty
And privilege to warm

The chill of death and fear
With the quickening wonder
That sounds and sparkles here
Like sunlight and like thunder...

The mighty harmonies
Of the body, born
Of spirit-mysteries —
The choiring victories
Of transmuted destinies —
In the eternal dawn."

Arvia MacKaye Ege

Where shall we wander, you and I,
Now death has flung his shadow here so high?
As once on Alpine mountainslopes we fled
The shadow of the evening peaks, and led
Each other up into the sun's warm ray,
Now ever upward I must shift my way,
Stalked by death-shadow, into spirit shine,

Till in that Alpine light I hear you say:
Death is a door through dark to the divine.
Climb higher still and wait till I can teach
Your heart to hear and hold my spirit speech.

Christy Barnes

The sorrow is so great
Each morning when I wake,
It seems as though my heart
Would break apart,
My being burst asunder,
With the echoes of the rending grandeur
Of the heavenly drama
Being now enacted,
Where you are newly born,
Just under
The fragile veil
Of our unwitting slumber.

Like the chastening flash
And impact of starry lightning,
Speaking with the pealing voice
And cleansing clash
Of cosmic thunder,
Its echoes roll
Beneath the brittle surface
Of our blatant everyday —

Leaving,
In the pent stillness of their wake,
Like potent balm
In the vast gulf of grief,
A breath of fresh inpouring wonder,

A swift intake
Of pure rejuvenating air —
Hushed anticipation,
Glistening, listening,
Gleaming,
In the newness —
Everywhere.

Arvia MacKaye Ege

FOR MY MOTHER

Many years after her death.

It is not hard to feel you near,
The air around you is so clear,
For you are selfless through and through.
Your being sparkles in the blue
Like sunrise rays through showers of dew.
How fresh your fragrance round you blows
Like breezes round a summer rose!
At home within your sun I bask;
More blessedness no child could ask.

Christy Barnes

The soul, true poetess, shall never die!
She is the whisper in all lovely things,
God's underlying mighty thunderings,
The holy of holies of the very I
of man enshrined within the starry sky,
and when she utters, all creation sings,
rejoicing in the light that lends us wings
and lets its spirit, liberated, fly.

Filled with deep pity for the unredeemed,
In sacrificial self-forgetfulness,
she hastens to the very deepest hell
and sets up her abode in darks undreamed,
risking her future life, no more, no less,
in seeing ways of making evil well.

Rex Raab
For A.M.E.

FOR
ARVIA MACKAYE EGE

January 4, 1989.

As silver
Moon vessels sailing,
Your words are ever
Borne billowing
In wisdom's winds
On waves eternal.

Bearing, Oh glorious:
Sun-fire,
Sacrifice —
Love.

As golden
Meteor vessels flaming,
Your words are ever
Toning in time's
Ranging rhythms,
Sounding
"The Secret Iron of the Heart."

O soul of spirit spheres,
May your burning
Ship set sail
Towards the shining sea
Of the midnight Sun!

Saskia Barnes

55

WHITE BIRDS IN FLIGHT

Christ, whom I love, is Lord of all that weaves and
        moves:
White birds in flight that scour my soul's horizon clean
and fiery, mountain-moving words,
receding rainbows, sunlight shimmering
        and dew that glints upon the petals of a rose —
Christ lives in them and he is never still.
The water-drops that rise and vanish —
Cloudlike, Christ condenses with them and his being
        showers the land.
He lives in thirsting earth and rushing air and trickling
        stream.
He is the water and the wind, the dancer and the dream,
the form and fire
of love he is. And he is present in the soul's desire
and in the ocean's deeply sighing breath.

Christ takes the corpse that rides upon my back
and throws it laughing to the wandering wind.
Upon my dried-out, parasitic head
he is the watering light.
His presence gently is precipitated
        into weaving images that bridge and heal.
He is the living liquid fountain that restores my soul,
the god of moving water, bubbling brook and rushing
        stream.
And as white birds in flight
have brought my weary, prodigal soul to rest at last in
        him,

so always go his messengers in manifold moving dress
          about the world
and call us out of movement
into active stillness,
peace and rest.

                                        Michael Burton
                                        For A.M.E.

Who tends the rosebush every spring
with so much love and care?
It is the dead who do this thing —
It is their glance and glistening
that fill the fragrant air.

At evening when the silence tones,
and you go deep inside —
the empty house is all your own,
your soul is used to being alone,
your gaze becomes more wide —

Then softest shine enkindles bright
your being, by and by,
and you are ready to invite
your friends out of the fair twilight
as heavenly company.

                                        Emma Krell-Werth

WHEN THE DEAD LOOK DOWN

When the dead look down
Into the waves and weathers of our souls,
What do they see?

Troubled cloud, despondent grey delay,
Dismay,
The fret and petty flutter of the mind
About a thousand splintered things?

Or do they breathe a sunny air that sings —
Gaze into quiet lakes of heart
That mirror stars and their own eyes,
Devout surprise?
And do they know again through us
The dance of windy leaves and daffodils,
The long clear lonely lines that make
The music of the hills?

And do they taste the springs of cool content
When we find them in full acknowledgement?

When the dead look down,
Oh can they drink
The shining thoughts we think?

Christy Barnes

FLOWER LANGUAGE

She who had died
Leaned down and cried,
"This hyacinth
I reach to you."
And I replied,
"What does it teach?"

"Each," she said,
"May from it learn
Wonder, reverence and love.
As fragrances from flowers rise,
So thanks and love up through your eyes.

"To the bells of blossoms ringing
Listen, for the dead are bringing
Through the silence starry singing.
Look into this tender blue;
It will make you pure and true.

"Sky-blue flowers you too will give
When you die to those who live.
    Heart's-rose-red
    Are for the dead."

Christy Barnes

Come!
Dear one, who wakes over yonder,
　　I will sing you a song: —
Through my eyes, through my heart,
Look at our garden
And see there
　　The joy of the opening flowers
　　You have loved for so long;

Hear there, within *me*,
　　The breathing tones of their colors,
　　The weaving harmonies
　　　　Of the lilies, the roses, the phlox,
　　Bright black-eyed susans and spires of yucca
　　　　Chiming with lupines and purple bells —
　　　　　　The high sigh of the trees,
　　　　　　The bass notes of the rocks;

They now burst here once more into bloom,
　　Greeting the day
　　In this sun-bathed, heaven-revealing disarray —
　　　The miracle and glory,
　　　　The mysterious story,
　　　　Of our dear rambling,
　　　　　　Clambering
　　　　　　Garden.

All of the rhythmical wonder
Played by star-fingered beings
    On the strings of the light and the air,
    On the trumpets, the pipes and the drums
      Of wind and water and earth.
    Where the world is fed
    And life is led
      In the intimate detection
      Of the resurrection.

Ah, how sweet the garden smells
As so it sings and tells: —
    Through all that you perceive through me
    And I receive through you,
      Through all we do
      Together, in such wise,
      We work upon the gleaming key
        To unlock the mystery
        Of paradise.

Arvia MacKaye Ege

Oh, look within the blossom's cup
until you know the lore of life.
You utter so for all the dead
the word that lets them love the earth,
and to the living give the light
that ripens heaven's wisdom here.

Yet but for Him who woke from death
you fill the blossom's brim no more —
with draught of memory no more —
and never with oblivion's dew.
Oh, learn yourself what flowers are,
Be chalice for the Living Sun.

Albert Steffen

POETS OF THE PAST

from Holy Sonnets

10

Death, be not proud, though some have calléd thee
Mighty and dreadful, for thou are not so;
For those whom thou think'st thou dost overthrow
Die not, poor Death, nor yet canst thou kill me.
From rest and sleep, which but thy pictures be,
Much pleasure; then from thee much more must flow,
And soonest our best men with thee do go,
Rest of their bones, and soul's delivery.
Thou'rt slave to fate, chance, kings, and desperate men,
And dost with poison, war, and sickness dwell,
And poppy or charms can make us sleep as well
And better than thy stroke; why swell'st thou then?
One short sleep past, we wake eternally
And death shall be no more; Death, thou shalt die.

John Donne

CHORUS OF THE DEAD

Oh we, the dead, we, the dead — far more are we
Than you on the earth, than you on the sea!
We plough the vast croplands with tireless deeds.
You reap with your scythes what has grown from our
        seeds,
And what we achieved, and what we've begun,
It pours still up yonder in the streams of the sun.
And all of our loving, our hating, our pains,
It beats still up yonder in death-endured veins:
With all the true treasures we've gathered and found
All earthly behaviour forever is bound.
With our sounding, our forming, our singing, we fight
To capture the crown of the outstreaming light,
Seeking ever the goal of mankind become free —
So revere us — and sacrifice! — Many are we.

Conrad Ferdinand Meyer

From

ADONAIS

XLI

He lives, he wakes — 'tis Death is dead, not he;
Mourn not for Adonais. — Thou young Dawn,
Turn all thy dew to splendour, for from thee
The spirit thou lamentest is not gone;
Ye caverns and ye forests, cease to moan!
Cease, ye faint flowers and fountains, and thou Air,
Which like a mourning veil thy scarf hadst thrown
O'er the abandoned Earth, now leave it bare
Even to the joyous stars which smile on its despair!

XLII

He is made one with Nature: there is heard
His voice in all her music, from the moan
Of thunder, to the song of night's sweet bird;
He is a presence to be felt and known
In darkness and in light, from herb and stone,
Spreading itself where'er that Power may move
Which has withdrawn his being to its own;
Which wields the world with never-wearied love,
Sustains it from beneath, and kindles it above....

The One remains, the many change and pass;
Heaven's light forever shines, Earth's shadows fly;
Life, like a dome of many coloured glass,
Stains the white radiance of Eternity,
Until Death tramples it to fragments....

LIV

That Light whose smile kindles the Universe,
That Beauty in which all things work and move,
That Benediction which the eclipsing Curse
Of birth can quench not, that sustaining Love
Which through the web of being blindly wove
By man and beast and earth and air and sea,
Burns bright or dim, as each are mirrors of
The first for which all thirst; now beams on me,
Consuming the last clouds of cold mortality.

LV

The breath whose might I have invoked in song
Descends on me; my spirit's bark is driven,
Far from the shore, far from the trembling throng
Whose sails were never to the tempest given;

The massy earth and spheréd skies are riven!
I am borne darkly, fearfully, afar;
Whilst, burning through the inmost veil of Heaven,
The soul of Adonais, like a star,
Beacons from the abode where the Eternal are.

P.B. Shelley

DEATH CAROL

from *When Lilacs Last in the Door-yard Bloom'd*

Come, lovely and soothing Death,
Undulate round the world, serenely arriving, arriving,
In the day, in the night, to all, to each,
Sooner or later, delicate Death.

Prais'd be the fathomless universe,
For life and joy, and for objects and knowledge curious:
And for love, sweet love — But praise! praise! praise!
For the sure-enwinding arms of cool-enfolding Death.

Dark Mother, always gliding near, with soft feet,
Have none chanted for thee a chant of fullest welcome?
Then I chant it for thee — I glorify thee above all;
I bring thee a song that when thou must indeed come,
        come unfalteringly.

Approach, strong Deliveress!
When it is so — when thou hast taken them, I joyously
        sing the dead,
Lost in the loving, floating ocean of thee,
Laved in the flood of thy bliss, O Death.

From me to thee glad serenades,
Dances for thee I propose, saluting thee — adornments
        and feastings for thee;

And the sights of the open landscape, and the high-
    spread sky, are fitting,
And life and the fields, and the huge and thoughtful
    night.

The night, in silence, under many a star;
The ocean shore, and the husky whispering wave, whose
    voice I know;
And the soul turning to thee, O vast and well-veil'd
    Death,
And the body gratefully nestling close to thee.

Over the tree-tops I float thee a song!
Over the rising and sinking waves — over the myriad
    fields, and the prairies wide;
Over the dense-pack'd cities all, and the teeming
    wharves and ways,
I float this carol with joy, with joy to thee, O Death!

Walt Whitman

A CREED

I hold that when a person dies
His soul returns again to earth:
Arrayed in some new flesh-disguise,
Another mother gives him birth.
With sturdier limbs and brighter brain
The old soul takes the road again.

Such was my belief and trust;
This hand, this hand that holds the pen,
Has many a hundred times been dust
And turned, as dust, to dust again;
These eyes of mine have blinked and shone
In Thebes, in Troy, in Babylon....

I know that in my lives to be
My sorry heart will ache and burn,
And worship unavailingly
The woman whom I used to spurn,
And shake to see another have
The love I spurned, the love she gave.

And I shall know, in angry words,
In gibes, and mocks, and many a tear,
A carrion flock of homing birds,
The gibes and scorns I uttered here.
The brave word that I failed to speak
Will brand me dastard on the cheek.

And as I wander on the roads
I shall be helped and healed and blessed;
Kind words shall cheer and be as goads
To urge to heights before unguessed.
My road shall be the road I made
All that I give shall be repaid.

So shall I fight, so shall I tread,
In the long war beneath the stars;
So shall a glory wreathe my head,
So shall I faint and show the scars,
Until this case, this clogging mould,
Be smithied all to kingly gold.

John Masefield

IN TIME OF WAR

You, who were slain so young,
Take, through my eyes, the redness of this rose,
The molten shimmer of the lake
Beneath the summer sky.

Take, through my love,
The light of this day on earth
To be with you in the land of the shades
Until you reach the Kingdom of the Sun.

Eleanor Trives

THE THRESHOLD CROSSED IN WAR

In October, 1914 I returned to Munich. My first experience in this German city (I will express it as directly and simply as I experienced it) was the nearness of the dead. I felt as if I lay in a damp, cold mass grave. But in this grim atmosphere of the graveyard, was also — the nearness to God, in the moment one summoned one's thinking to activity. I felt that the decay of the body, which is a necessity of nature, can, in no way, hamper the liberation of the spirit. Never had I experienced dying and becoming so closely intertwined.

When I stood by one of those pillars on which the telegrams were posted reporting the course of the battle, I sensed not only the stream of blood that had flowed but also the powers of inspiration that the spiritual world had poured out over mankind. Those fallen in war, whose death was a sacrifice, wanted to speak of love to those they had left behind. The bridge between the living and the dead was there. It only needed to be set foot upon....

I remember a performance of Mozart's *Requiem*. One knows the legend that is associated with the origin of this work. An unknown stranger comes to the composer and commissions him to create a memorial for the dead. Mozart, who already carried the seed of his own death in him, began to create with his last strength. The stranger was Death who called him away to higher deeds.

The chorus was sung by brothers and sisters of soldiers who had fallen on the battle front. All came dressed in black. The tones created a rainbow path into the spirit. An indestructible road over which friend and foe might pass. The temple to which it led was for everyone, built for men of the West, of the East and of Middle Europe.

I experienced the certainty that evening that a community to which the dead do not belong will never last.

The dead are not bound by national boundaries.

It was at this time that I read in a German newspaper about the graves on the Oise; the wooden crosses of fallen German soldiers had been decorated with roses. Below stood the inscription: *"Offert par les Francaises aux soldats allemands, nos frères en Jesus Christ...."*

Albert Steffen

OUTGROWN

Two heart-broken parents who had recently lost their son in the war, and were bravely trying to console his young wife and child, were aroused one night to find him bending over them.

They hardly recognized him at first, he had grown so much bigger, more powerful, and though it hardly seemed possible, even nobler and more handsome than when they had seen him last. It was by the gleam in his eyes that they knew him at once, for that was unmistakable. Yet the depth of expression in his glance startled them, and they were awed by the maturity and grandeur that hovered about his boyish features.

In his arms he was carrying a strange bundle. It might have been a crumpled parachute, or an old battle-coat, and resembled, oddly enough, a great cocoon. Peering closer, however, they saw that its folds glowed with vivid, many-colored images and realized that it was the life which he had just laid aside.

"It was too small," he said, holding it out for them to see. "I could not wear it any longer, it had grown so tight! The bursting shell only burst the last button that held it together. I am so sorry, for you gave it to me. But I have grown too big for it."

"You have indeed outgrown it," cried his father, gazing up at him in incredulous amazement.

"But how shall I make a new one?" asked his mother earnestly. "We have nothing that will even remotely fit nor anything that is fine or stout enough for you now."

"We shall have to spin and weave it from the beginning — all of us together," replied her son. "But first I shall have to shear and gather the wool from the lambs in the fields yonder."

He gazed off over the greening hillsides, and as he spoke they were aware of a wound in his breast. It glowed deeply red, disclosing to their wonderment the clustering petals of a crimson flower of extraordinary beauty.

"I will go to the pastures to seek the lambs for the shearing," he said. "But see — this will help to keep my little one warm."

Bending down, he tucked the outgrown garment closely about his baby boy, took the flower from his breast and, laying it gently upon the heart of his young wife where she slept, strode away — toward the green pastures.

Arvia MacKaye Ege

FROM AN AUTOBIOGRAPHY

In October, 1918 — I was just eighteen — we had hacked through the Argonne Forest and the Germans were falling back, leaving holding units.

Our patrol had to go ahead before dawn across a wide open space to a bombed-out village called Grand Prè. That's Great Meadow. We were supposed to clear out machine-gun nests that had been holding up the advance from a hillside above the town.... I don't remember much about getting there except it was raining and cold and we had to wade a small stream. I remember I was terribly afraid; almost numb with fear. I remember I had a strange fateful feeling about not coming back.

We got there safely, just before full daylight. I was in a stone house with hardly any roof at all when there came a grenade shower to precede a rushing attack down the slope. These German hand grenades — we called them potato mashers because of their shape — were not so deadly as ours. Deadly enough though, and the wooden handle flying through the air could knock your head right off.

When the first grenade shower came, I looked up and saw one strike a rafter a few feet directly above my head. I saw it wobble and fall and the strange thing was I was quite calm at the moment. "Free from fear at last," I thought, and to myself I said, "Well then, this is it. The end." But in that same instant — you could call it the twinkling of an eye, I suppose — I seemed to be immediately in a vast world of light infinitely far from where I had been a moment before. Everywhere this beautiful, radiant, limitless light and not a sound anywhere. Deep silence. Silence so complete it could be felt, almost seen, and the wonder of it was that I heard a voice coming from I couldn't tell where but from a great distance: coming through the silence but not disturbing it, and calling, "Look Up! Look Up!" I thought I had heard that voice before: a voice I knew well but couldn't think where I had known it.

Then, too, there before me as I stood in awe — funny thing, I couldn't tell either if this was close up or far, far away — anyhow there appeared right out of the light a beautiful cloudlike form and it seemed to be a *density*, a densification of the very light itself. I thought it must be an angel because it floated in air and bore me upward, as I thought, but really it was only my eyes that were lifted to the heavens. I stood perfectly still, I think, the whole time from beginning to end. But that doesn't matter because here and there, close up and far away were all the same it seemed to me.

So up there I saw a picture of weaving golden streams against the pale blue of the sky. I saw two figures there in front. One of them was Hugh, my dearest friend, who had fallen at my side only a few days earlier. Hugh was smiling, not sadly, but wistfully, it seemed, on the other figure who — in a sudden flash as the picture began to fade just a little, I saw, wonder to behold, — was myself.

Then slowly the whole scene with the angel figure began to recede and as they faded, I heard the voice out of the silence. But now it seemed to be a great shout, a deluge of sound, calling — "WE LIVE! WE LIVE!"

I stood there straining to see and hear more as the call, repeated, grew fainter with each repetition; watching the scene dissolve back into the ethereal light.... Until what I suppose must have been the explosion of the grenade knocked me into unconsciousness, into oblivion....

The next thing I knew I was lying on a stretcher raised just off the ground. I looked steadily, for I don't know how many minutes, at a long downward sweep of dirty canvas. There was a tear in it halfway up and I watched a drip-drip-drip. All around me on the wet grass were other stretchers with figures under blankets. In a little while I knew where I was — under the tent of a Field Hospital.

Al Laney

LETTERS FROM A SOLDIER IN THE
TRENCHES TO HIS YOUNG PUPIL AT HOME

*The war had become stationary. Like millions of other soldiers,
Dr. Curtius was dug in at the front and made use of the endless
weeks to write to his former pupil.*

Amongst other things, Dr. Curtius wrote:

Life first acquires meaning when we have before us
in spirit those who have given their lives in sacrifice.
They ask continually, "Why have we departed from life?
And for what end? Have you transformed yourselves
since we sacrificed our lives? Without asking many
questions we went to our death, for your future. We
had confidence that afterwards you would wrestle for
the meaning of dying, which we ourselves did not know.
What have you achieved?"

But these questions of the dead only amount to the
following: "Will you not perceive and receive our in-
sight which we have won in the realm of the spirit?"

Impelling impulses reach those who are left behind.
They come more especially from those among the fallen
who passed through the gates of death in their first
youth. They passed through as lovers, without question
of reward; just because of this they have attained over
there the radiance of the spirit. But because they still
bear within them fresh earthly powers of growth, they
press close to us, the living, with their gift. They wish
to give what once would have become accomplished

work. They do not want to let these seeds spoil and come to nothing, but seek human hearts wherein to plant them. Oh, see the souls of the early departed! They come and sit down beside the young poet, who wakes with a pure heart, and lead his hand; they come to the young musician and whisper in his ear, and to lovers who incline trustingly toward one another.

"What shall I do?" I ask every night; and every morning I find answer. Are science, the state, the church, which cannot prevent this bath of blood, then sufficient? The melancholy with which I awaken in the morning says repeatedly, "no."

In the evening I ask, "Tell me, my dear friend, what you desire of me?" In the morning the answer within me is, "You must tread the path to us, the unborn and the immortal, that we may give you the power of the spirit."

And I exercise my soul throughout the day upon the plant world, which is pure, that I may become selfless like itself; yet not sleep, but waken.

When I immerse myself in the green which lies spread out before me, I feel myself lifted up into a rosy life-element. A freshness, which does not arise from my physical body, steals through me and blesses me. Hunger and thirst, all bodily feelings vanish. Even the weariness of death has lost its power. I am cleansed. A feeling of redemption flows into me. I know that it comes from the Son of the Sun.

*

The souls of those fallen in battle had lived in madness, they had hated and killed; they wandered now in the memory of what they had done, journeying backwards, perceiving everything in that light which had now become for them like eyes. For dying is a shedding of light over the landscape of life. Such a sunrise of the selves was an unveiling that elevated, ordered and judged, was a destruction of the destructive, a seeking to make good every evil. — The more inexorably the soul purifies itself, the more invincible becomes its radiance. This life is the sweetest life of the dead.

Because within the human soul itself the battle for the freedom of the ego was not carried through and won, the outer battle had to begin and blood to flow. Through knowledge which is schooled in the light of Christ, the demon must be cast forth from the blood. No longer may the blood be the bearer of race instincts, but only the ego, which through the power of knowledge lovingly experiences the entire human race. The soul still continues to live with the motion that throbbed in the blood while it still pulsed in the organism even after it has slipped from the body; it ascends in the form of a lemniscate to the stars, to Moon, Mercury, Venus, Sun, Mars, Jupiter, Saturn, ascends aloft into the entire Cosmic All, only to return at length to the earth.

I feel myself carried forth by the multifold stream of life which ascends from the earth into the heavens, flows from star to star, circling through the entire cosmos. I understand the surge of its waves because I live within the souls of the dead, whom I loved.

Often it is for me as if the radiance of the tide were the light of innumerable eyes.

The blood by means of which life pulses throughout the whole of humanity is only alive because the God-head lives within the whole. The heart of Christ beats for all. What an overwhelming thought that once a human being lived who bore the pulse-beat of humanity through death. This rhythm is immortal and alive henceforth upon earth. Human beings cannot pause until they have recognized him and made him their own. They sense that continually something within them says: Do not rest until you have reached the center of humanity. It lies there where the earth becomes sun, in the heart. Nowhere else. Only there are freedom and love one, for everyone. Here seek the Christ.

Whosoever feels the pulse-beat of the whole of humanity knows also how he must stand in relationship to the dead.

Albert Steffen

From CHORAL REQUIEM
FOR THOSE FALLEN IN WAR

Chorus of All the Living

For the grave,
for grief,
for virtue,
for sacrifice,
hold thy body fortified.

By the earth,
by the water,
by the air,
by the light,
shall the soul be purified.

To death,
to the Judge,
to the Creator,
to the Christus,
let the spirit be thy guide.

Albert Steffen